Attitude of Gratitude Book from A to Z

Enjoy life..........Life is not a practice, it is real.

I wrote this book to inspire not just children but also adults to remember to be grateful for each day and all that is around them. We all have one life; we should enjoy it and appreciate life as well as others around us.

I encourage everyone to look around and be grateful for what you have and who you are. Everyone is just as important and the next person.

.

I would like to thank my husband for encouraging me to be the best I can be. Also, my three wonderful daughters, for being patient while I complete this book.

Aa

dventure

DAY IN THE SKY!

Bb

EAUTIFUL

AS A BUTTERFLY.

Cc

SOMEONE IS

CARING FOR

ME.

Dd

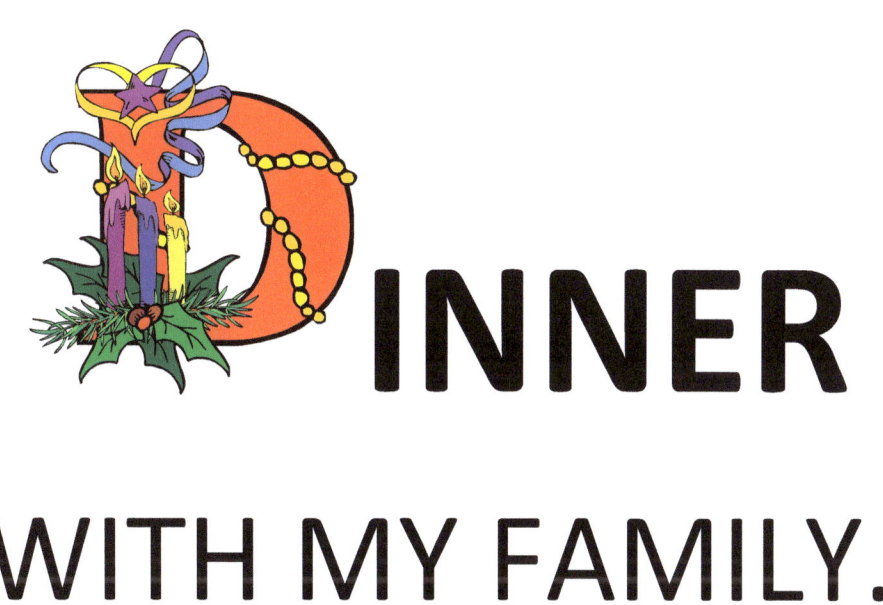

INNER

WITH MY FAMILY.

Ee

EARTH THAT WE LIVE ON.

Ff

FLOWERS IN

THE GARDEN.

Gg

RATEFUL

TO BE ALIVE.

Hh

APPINESS

IS ENJOYING BEING

WITH OTHERS.

Ii

 LOVE YOU!

Jj

OY OF

LIFE.

Kk

**NOWLEDGE IS POWER.**

LI

EARNING

NEVER GIVE UP.

Mm

OVIE NIGHT

WITH A FRIEND!

Nn

ICE WALK

IN THE PARK.

Oo

PENING THE DOOR TO A SURPRISE!

Pp

LAYING

ON THE SHORE OF A

BEACH.

Qq

UIET TIME

WHEN IT IS TIME TO GO TO BED.

Rr

RACE. TO

THE FINISH LINE.

Ss

URPRISES

DURING THE

HOLIDAYS!

Tt

TEACHERS

TEACH EVERYONE.

Uu

P THE

LADDER TO SUCCESS!

Vv

 **OICE** TO

SING.

Ww

WATERFALL SOUNDS ARE PEACEFUL.

Xx

-**RAY** MY PUPPY, I THINK HE ATE MY TOY.

Yy

OU'RE MY

BEST FRIEND.

Zz

LET'S GO TO THE

OO!

www.ingramcontent.com/pod-product-compliance
Lightning Source LLC
Chambersburg PA
CBHW041508280526
45792CB00004B/1181